IN

Alan Fowler has worked widely in both the private and public sectors, with personnel appointments in four industries and two local authorities. He is now a freelance consultant, a director of Personnel Publications Ltd, and a member of the editorial board of *People Management,* the fortnightly journal of the IPD. He writes extensively on personnel issues, with regular articles in *People Management* and the *Local Government Chronicle.* His books for the IPD include *The Disciplinary Interview* (1996) and *Negotiating, Persuading and Influencing* (1995), both in the Management Shapers series; *Negotiating Skills and Strategies* (second edition 1996); *Get More – and More Results – from Your People* (1998); *Get More – and More Value – from Your People* (1998); and *Managing Redundancy* (1999). All these titles are available from the IPD.

042724

The Institute of Personnel and Development is the leading publisher of books and reports for personnel and training professionals, students, and all those concerned with the effective management and development of people at work. For details of all our titles, please contact the Publishing Department:

tel 020-8263 3387

fax 020-8263 3850

e-mail publish@ipd.co.uk

The catalogue of all IPD titles can be viewed on the IPD website:

www.ipd.co.uk

INDUCTION

ALAN FOWLER

INSTITUTE OF PERSONNEL AND DEVELOPMENT

Design and typesetting by
Wyvern 21, Bristol

Printed in Great Britain by
the Short Run Press, Exeter

British Library Cataloguing-in-Publication Data
A catalogue record for this book is available
from the British Library

ISBN 0-85292-814-9

INSTITUTE OF PERSONNEL
AND DEVELOPMENT

IPD House, Camp Road, Wimbledon, London SW19 4UX
Tel.: 020-8971 9000   Fax: 020-8263 3333
Registered office as above. Registered Charity No. 1038333
A company limited by guarantee. Registered in England No. 2931892

Contents

Other titles in the series

What is induction and why is it important?

> ☑ The costs of early leaving
> ☑ Elements of induction

Whenever new employees join an organisation there is always a period of learning and adaptation before they become fully effective. Partly, this involves finding out about the practicalities of the job and facts about pay, other employee benefits and the organisation's rules and regulations. But there is also the need to understand the less tangible but very powerful influence of 'the way we do things around here'. Every organisation has its own style or culture and new employees are unlikely to be fully effective or feel comfortable in their work until they have absorbed this cultural influence and adjusted to it.

In a very general sense, induction is this process of initial learning and adjustment, whether or not the process is planned or structured by the employer. In organisations that provide no form of induction, many new staff may eventually settle in, relying on their own efforts to learn about the organisation and with informal help from their colleagues. But there are two major risks involved in leaving induction to chance.

- The process is likely to take far longer than if induction was planned, and this slow learning period carries hidden costs.
- Not all new entrants will learn and adapt successfully, and the organisation is then likely to experience the significant disruption and costs of replacing early leavers.

The costs of early leaving

Many employees who leave soon after joining an organisation do so because they have not been helped either to understand their role or to adapt to the organisational culture – both aspects being central to effective induction. Many studies of employee turnover have shown that:

- in almost all organisations, resignations are most frequent among employees with less than one year's service
- the higher the turnover rate, the larger the proportion of leavers within their first few weeks or months of employment
- organisations that operate an intensive period of initial training generally experience very low levels of early leaving.

Results like these suggest that although some early leaving may be the unavoidable result of the process of personal adjustment by which people ultimately find jobs that suit them, its incidence can be significantly reduced by positive action. Why does this matter? There are two principal reasons: the costs of finding and training replacement employees; and the damage to the organisation's reputation as an employer of a high rate of early leaving. Any reduction in turnover cuts recruitment and training costs, but action that reduces early leaving is particularly cost effective.

An employee who resigns after, say, six years' service will have justified the costs of recruitment and initial training, but when someone leaves after only three months, there will be no payback for these costs. Halving the early leaving rate for, say, a workforce of 500 telesales staff with an overall current turnover rate of 35 per cent, of which 50 per cent leave in their first six months, could save at least £100,000 a year. Of course, skilful selection and a reasonably attractive package of pay and conditions contribute to staff retention, but well-planned induction has a major role to play.

An organisation that experiences a high incidence of employees leaving during their first few months may also acquire a reputation as a poor employer. Early leavers are often disillusioned and tend to put all the blame on the organisation – even if in some cases they may themselves have failed to put sufficient effort into making a success of their new jobs. Most are likely to tell friends and family that the organisation was a bad employer, and a reputation of this kind will spread and make it increasingly difficult to recruit good-quality staff. One aim of an effective induction policy is to generate enthusiasm for working for the organisation, and this enhances its employment reputation.

Elements of induction

Induction is therefore a planned and systematic process, structured and implemented by the organisation, to help new employees settle into their new jobs quickly, happily and effectively. There is much more to it than the running of formal induction courses, useful though these are. The longer-term process of tuning in to the style of the organisation and understanding its aims and values cannot be achieved by simply attending a course. New employees bring with them expectations about the job and the organisation, gained through the organisation's reputation and by contact during the recruitment and selection process – so parts of that process need to be treated as pre-induction. How the new employee is received on the first day at work creates a strong first impression and so requires particular attention. Also, the way supervisors and managers behave in their day-to-day contacts with their staff has a major influence on how well and how quickly new employees settle in.

It is also important to recognise that existing employees who transfer or who are promoted within the organisation require help in settling into their new jobs, as do those returning to work after lengthy career breaks. Home-based employees and part-timers are often omitted from formal induction programmes, but their needs for assistance in adjusting to new working circumstances can be considerable. So induction should not be limited to new recruits to full-time jobs. It is necessary, too, for induction to reflect the specific characteristics of different types of work and of different economic sectors. A thorough and well-planned approach to induction carries dividends to the employer in helping to secure a competent, motivated workforce; and it benefits the individual employee by contributing positively to career development.

> KEY POINTS
> - Induction is a planned, systematic process to help new employees settle into their jobs quickly, happily and effectively.
> - Effective induction reduces the time and cost of the initial learning and adjustment period and minimises the number of early leavers.

How is induction influenced by the recruitment process?

☑ The job advertisement
☑ The selection process
☑ Pre-employment documentation

All new employees start work with some expectations and preconceptions about their new jobs. The accuracy or inaccuracy of these ideas – many of which are gained during the recruitment process – can have a significant effect on employee turnover during the first few weeks of employment. If the job proves much less attractive in reality than the impression given during recruitment, the consequent disillusionment may well trigger a resignation. More positively, some preparation for assimilation into the new job can be achieved before the first day at work, and so expedite the later induction process. This has implications for:

- the design and content of the job advertisement
- how selection testing and interviewing are conducted

- the issue and nature of pre-employment documentation.

The job advertisement

First impressions about an employer may well derive from the style and content of job advertisements. Their purpose is to generate applications and it is consequently logical for them to highlight the attractive features of the job; but with induction in mind, it is important that the image created by the advertisement and the reality that new employees will experience are compatible. Advertisements which may result in large numbers of applicants but which can cause induction problems are likely to include one or more of the following flaws:

- over-optimistic statements about the potential for high earnings
- unrealistic promises about career development opportunities
- descriptions of the work as 'challenging' or 'exciting', when much of it is repetitive and prescriptive routine
- pictorial representations of the workplace which give a false impression of the working environment
- claims about equal opportunities which are not supported by employees' everyday working experience.

Advertisements that attract good applicants and help to set the scene for eventual new employees usually have the following characteristics:

- a general style of design and advertising copy which reflects the culture of the organisation
- an emphasis on the aspects of the work from which effective employees derive particular satisfaction
- accuracy about pay and conditions, and about any significant requirements such as mobility or the need to work unsocial hours.

There is steadily growing use of the Internet for recruitment, and this offers the opportunity to provide extensive pre-employment information to prospective applicants. Websites can include far more information in both pictorial and text form about an organisation and its activities than can a conventional job advertisement in the printed media. Additionally, some organisations using the Internet for recruitment provide the e-mail addresses of various existing employees and invite potential applicants to contact these staff on an informal basis with any questions they wish about the organisation and what it is like to work there. These e-mail contacts may be employees in any function – they are not the formal personnel department contacts. Imaginative use of the Internet can help to ensure that job applicants already have a good understanding of the nature of the organisation and that, if selected, they will bring to their new jobs an accurate impression of what working life will be like.

The selection process

How applicants are treated during selection testing and interviewing will have a powerful influence on their perceptions and expectations. Here, for the first time, the potential new employee has a personal contact with the potential employer, and may see the workplace and meet the immediate manager. Of course, if selection is limited to a single interview, conducted by a personnel officer off site, say at a local hotel, with no supporting documentation and followed by a letter of appointment, new employees will be almost as ignorant of what the job is really like as they were when they first saw the job advertisement.

At the other extreme, candidates may be grouped for an initial talk about the organisation, given a tour of the establishment, then interviewed by both a personnel specialist and their potential line managers, and provided with company literature and adequate opportunities to ask questions. Candidates handled in this way are able to self-select to the extent that those who feel they would not be happy in the organisation can pull out of the selection process – thereby reducing the possible incidence of early leavers.

Some care is needed in the way selection testing is dealt with. A false impression about an organisation can be given by the use of selection tests which project an image of the organisation that differs from reality – for example, by creating an impression of a formal and highly sophisticated approach when the organisation itself has a very informal and down-to-earth culture. There needs also to be a reasonable degree of face validity about tests – that is, candidates should be able to see the relevance of what they are asked to do, rather than being mystified, irritated or even upset by what might be perceived as irrelevant or intrusive test questions or activities.

How candidates are received when attending for selection purposes also contributes to their perception of the organisation. Confusion about times or where to report to, or being kept waiting for long periods in uncomfortable surroundings, are all examples of experiences which could make the new employee doubtful about the wisdom of having accepted the offer of an interview and create an impression that the induction process has to work hard to eradicate.

However, a highly efficient and candidate-friendly selection process carries the risk of later disillusionment unless induction into the job is similarly managed. If potential employees are looked after much better during selection than when they start work, some disappointment is inevitable. What this emphasises is the need for co-ordination of the whole process of recruitment, selection and induction, to make the most seamless transition possible from the interested but uncommitted candidate to the enthusiastic and effective new employee.

Pre-employment documentation

Once an applicant has been offered and accepted a job, four types of documents, issued before the new employee starts work, are relevant to effective induction:

- literature about the company
- details about the job – generally, the job description
- the terms and conditions of employment
- instructions about reporting for the first day at work.

Some general information about the organisation can be provided, either by issuing standard publicity literature or preferably in material written specifically for new employees. A question and answer format for a short introductory leaflet can be particularly helpful. It might have headings such as:

- *Who are we and what do we do?* This will give brief details about the organisation's role, the range of its activities, its size, and perhaps a little about its history.
- *What have we achieved and what are our aims?* This can highlight recent successes and explain the organisation's mission and key objectives.
- *What is it like to work with us?* This will describe and explain the organisation's core values and its general employment culture.
- *Where are we and what are the local facilities?* This can provide information about public transport access, together with details about shops, restaurants, leisure clubs and the like, which employees can go to during lunch breaks or before or after work.

The job description may already have been issued to candidates during the selection process. If not, it can be included in the information pack sent to new employees before they start work. If it is to be issued at this stage, it is important that information provided about the job during selection is fully consistent with the job description. Brief standard job descriptions for whole categories of work may need to be supplemented by additional information about the particular job involved.

Although legislation permits statements of terms and conditions of employment to be issued after employees have started work, it is much better practice to include them with formal offers or confirmations of employment. Because of the need to comply with both statute and contract law, these documents are generally written in very formal terminology. It can be helpful to accompany them with a much more friendly and informally written leaflet which explains the pay and conditions and can also cover points (such as the organisation's smoking policy) which do not have to be notified statutorily. To protect the organisation's legal position, a leaflet of this kind may need to include a statement to the effect that:

> The purpose of this leaflet is to help new employees understand the details of the organisation's conditions of employment, but does not itself form part of the contract of employment.

New employees need clear instructions about where and when to report on their first day at work. These instructions, outlined in the following check-list, should be explicit about the many basic details which the new employee will worry about if the requirements are unclear.

- *Reporting time:* it can be helpful to set this a little after the normal start time to ensure that reception staff and supervisors are present when the new employee arrives.
- *Place:* which entrance to use; or if reporting to a department, the location or room number.
- *Person to report to:* who the new employee should ask for when reporting to reception.
- *Car parking:* if relevant, where the new employee may park.

- *Clothing:* any rules about a dress code or the issue of protective clothing.
- *Security:* any information needed to gain access to the reporting location, such as a pass to show to the security staff on the gate.
- *Catering:* information about the availability of catering facilities, so the new employee knows whether or not it is necessary to bring a lunch or go out for the lunch break.
- *Medical check:* if a medical check is involved on the first day, brief details of its nature and purpose.
- *Documents:* A reminder to bring any necessary documents, such as the P45, a signed copy of the contract of employment, driving licence or birth certificate.
- *Arrangements for the day:* an outline of what will happen during the day, perhaps including a reminder that the morning will be spent on an induction course.

Pre-employment induction will have served its purpose if the new employee can look forward to the first day of work without any major worries about what to do on arrival or what is to happen during the day. On going home at the end of this first day, the employee's family and friends are likely to ask: 'What was it like ?' If pre-employment induction has been effective, the answer should be something like: 'OK – very much what I expected.'

KEY POINTS

- New employees start work with impressions and expectations acquired during the recruitment process and these impressions need to be realistic if disillusionment is to be avoided. Elements of the recruitment process therefore need to be addressed when planning induction.

- Job advertisements need to project an image consistent with the organisation's style or culture, and provide accurate information about the work, pay and conditions.

- Job advertising on the Internet offers an opportunity to provide potential applicants with far more information than can be given in conventional job advertisements.

- The way job applicants are treated during selection influences their perception of the organisation and needs to be handled in a way which contributes to a seamless transition from job applicant to new employee.

- Four types of documents to provide basic initial information can be issued before a newly recruited employee starts work :
  - literature about the organisation
  - the job description
  - terms and conditions of employment
  - instructions about reporting for work on the first day.

- Practical details about where, when and to whom to report help the new employee to overcome apprehension about the first day at work.

What should be included in the first day's induction?

- ✔ The initial reception
- ✔ Documentation
- ✔ The 'must know' items
- ✔ Who does what

However well-prepared the new starter may be, some nervousness about the first day in a new job is inevitable. There are so many things to experience and learn about – the geography of the work site, the daily work routines, who the managers and colleagues are and how they behave, rules and regulations about safety and security – questions about all these points and many more will be running through the mind of the new starter as he or she travels to the workplace for the first time.

A well-planned first day, starting with initial reception arrangements, is an essential feature of an effective induction programme – though it is also important to avoid too intensive a schedule. Everything cannot be dealt with in a single day, as new employees are not receptive to a great mass of information, particularly if much of it has little relevance to their overriding need to get through their first day without making embarrassing mistakes. The emphasis should therefore be on practical matters, such as the initial reception, the introduction to the workplace, learning the geography of the site, and an explanation of any immediately relevant safety or conduct requirements.

The initial reception

New employees should have been given clear instructions about when and where to report for work for the first time and what documents and other items to bring with them. The initial reception may involve reporting to a general reception desk, to the personnel department or to the actual workplace – perhaps to the manager's secretary. Whatever the precise arrangements, the following checklist can be used to ensure that things go smoothly:

- Set a reporting time that will ensure the availability of the people the new employee will first meet.
- Ensure that the person to whom the new employee must first report (and, if relevant, the security staff) knows of his or her impending arrival and what to do next.
- Train reception and security staff in the need for a friendly welcome and the efficient processing of any immediate administrative matters.
- Avoid keeping the new employee waiting: steady, unhurried activity is the best antidote for first-day nerves.

- Check whether the new employee has had any difficulties in making the journey to work on time, finding the site or the entrance, parking the car, and the like.
- If the new employee has to go to another location after initial reception, provide a guide.
- Ensure the new employee is introduced personally to whoever is taking over after initial reception.

Documentation

It is usually necessary to complete some form of documentation on the new employee's first day – often best done before the introduction to the workplace. Some documents may have to be produced by the employee; others may be issued by the employing organisation. Such items may include:

- From the employee:
    Income tax form P45
    Details of next of kin
    Details of GP (ie if medical checks are involved)
    Driving licence and car insurance
    Birth certificate (ie for pension purposes)
    Details of previous pension arrangements
    First aid certificate, if relevant
    Passport and work permit if not a UK citizen

- From the organisation:
    Staff handbook
    ID or security pass
    Clocking-in card or key
    Locker key

Staff restaurant or vending machine tokens
Car park entry card or permit
Authorisation to draw protective clothing or tools from store
Documentation for a company car
Safety rules and literature

If there is a large volume of material to be issued, thought should be given to issuing only the immediately necessary items on the first day and dealing with the remainder during the next few days.

The 'must know' items

Once the initial reception and documentation have been completed, attention should be given to the practical matters that the new employee needs to know about immediately. These are likely to include:

- the location of the employee's work site, and how to get to it from the staff entrance
- the location of the lavatories, cloakroom or lockers, vending machines or staff restaurant
- time-recording procedures
- times of rest and meal breaks
- any immediately applicable health and safety rules – including fire exits and matters such as a no-smoking policy or designated smoking areas; and arrangements, if applicable, for protective clothing
- the location and layout of the employee's personal work station and any related equipment
- any rules about the use of telephones or PCs

- any key points about conduct – particularly those related to the specific nature of the job, such as the handling of customer queries or complaints
- an introduction to the immediate supervisor or manager if he or she has not been involved in the initial reception
- introductions to immediate colleagues or members of the team the new employee is joining.

Unless new employees are scheduled to attend an induction course on their first day (see Chapter 6) it is also important to start them working as quickly as possible. There is nothing worse for a new employee than sitting at the work station with nothing to do, feeling embarrassedly isolated and conspicuous. The aim should be to keep the employee busy, but to start with the simple basics of the job. If formal job training is involved, the training programme should take in the more complex elements of the work on a phased basis over subsequent days.

Who does what

Except in very small and informal organisations, it is unlikely that all the first-day induction procedures will be handled by one person only. The precise arrangements as to who does what will obviously depend on the structure of each organisation, but at least five roles can be identified, which may either involve six people or be combined, at least in part:

- the receptionist or security officer
- the personnel officer

- the immediate supervisor or manager
- the senior manager
- a designated work colleague (the 'starter's friend')
- a job tutor.

The roles of *the receptionist and security staff* have been outlined in the preceding section about the initial reception.

If the first contact after arrival is with *the personnel officer*, it is at this point that most of the initial administrative matters can be dealt with. This is likely to include checking the P45 and other documents that the new employees have been asked to bring with them, and getting signatures for the receipt of ID cards, car park permits and other company documents. This is also the time to see if the new starter has any immediate problems or questions, and generally to set the helpful and welcoming tone for subsequent induction. It also provides the employee with a personal contact for later use if any problems arise which cannot be dealt with in the workplace. If the next step is for employees to proceed to the workplace, the personnel officer can take them there and introduce them to their immediate supervisors or managers.

It is essential that new employees are met at the workplace by *the supervisor or manager* to whom they will report and with whom they will consequently have daily contact. In many cases this person will have taken part in the selection process, so this will not then be a meeting of strangers. Otherwise, it is for the personnel officer to make the introduction. In either event, this is the first opportunity for the supervisor to establish the right rapport with his or her new staff member, and a friendly and positive approach at this point will do much to establish the supervisor's ongoing position. First impressions have a powerful influence on the quality of the employment relationship. The supervisor's primary role is to explain any essential dos and don'ts, settle new employees quickly into the workplace, introduce them to their new colleagues, ensure they can quickly start doing useful work (or start on a learning programme), and generally monitor during the remainder of the day that all is going according to plan.

Depending on the management structure, it may be appropriate for new employees to be introduced on their first day to *the senior manager* heading the particular department or function. This may involve little more than a handshake and a few words of welcome, but it can usefully add to a new employee's feeling of being wanted and recognised as an individual. Some senior managers make a particular point of meeting all new employees on their first day – partly so that they have seen who is joining the organisation but also to demonstrate that senior managers are not remote figures and do have an interest in everyone who works for the organisation.

Although immediate supervisors and managers have the primary responsibility for ensuring that new employees quickly settle in, they may well not have sufficient time personally to explain everything the new starter needs to know. It is consequently very helpful to designate one of the new employee's colleagues to act as a guide ('*starter's friend*'). This person, who needs to be carefully selected and briefed about this role, can show the new employee where everything is, make sure he or she understands the organisation's routines, and be generally helpful in explaining and advising on anything the new employee needs to know about. One advantage of this is that an experienced and perceptive colleague can explain the informal culture of the workplace, as well as dealing with the official rules and regulations. For example, tips about the informal dress code, where not to sit in the staff restaurant, and whether or not to use first names when talking to managers can help the new employee to avoid many potential embarrassments.

Formal job training is beyond the scope of this book, but if the new employee has first to embark on a course of such training, an early introduction to the *job tutor* will be necessary. Job tutors should be given full details about new starters so that it is unnecessary for them to ask for information that has already been collected. They should also be told about what elements of the induction programme have already been covered, and which are their responsibility. These may include, for example:

- the issue of equipment and protective clothing
- any health and safety matters that apply only to the training area and training activities
- the issue of procedure schedules or manuals.

Job training programmes should also take account of the need for a progression from the simpler to the more complex elements of the work, and the fact that people have different learning styles. For both the first day and subsequent induction stages, it is very helpful to use a check-list of everything the induction programme should cover and who is responsible for covering each item, and to have a record of its being done. An example is given in the Appendix.

KEY POINTS

- A well-planned first day, with the emphasis on explaining practical matters, is an essential feature of effective induction.

- Reception and security staff should be informed of new employees' arrival and trained in the correct way to receive them.

- Initial documentation needs to be completed before introducing the new employee to the workplace. This may include collecting documents and information from the employee (eg the P45 tax form) and issuing the employee with an ID pass and details of car parking, catering and other practical matters.

- The introduction to the workplace should on the first day concentrate on explaining the geography of the site, essential health and safety rules, time-recording procedures and similar 'must know' items.

- Unless new employees are to attend a first-day induction course, they should start working as soon as possible, with the aim of being kept busy with the simple basics of the job. Inactivity should be avoided.

- Several people are likely to be involved in first-day induction – reception staff, the personnel officer, the immediate supervisor or manager, a senior manager, a designated work colleague ('starter's friend') and a job tutor. Each needs to be clear about his or her particular induction role.

- It can be helpful to designate a work colleague to provide the new employee with friendly and informal assistance and advice.

- Both for the first day and in subsequent induction it is advisable to use a checklist of all the topics to be covered and who is to deal with each, by when.
- Avoid an overload of information on the first day by scheduling some matters for later explanation.

What should be planned after the first day?

> ☑ Knowledge of the organisation
> ☑ Understanding the employment package
> ☑ Social integration
> ☑ Progress reviews
> ☑ Probation

Once the first day at work has been completed, consideration can be given to extending the new employee's knowledge of the organisation beyond the immediate workplace
and the first essential aspects of the job. The whole process
of becoming acclimatised to a new job may take several
months, and an effective induction programme needs to
take this into account. What is wanted is a steady expansion
of understanding about how the organisation operates, the
employee's role within this, and the rights and obligations
involved in being an employee. Help with adjusting to the
organisation's culture is also needed. If culture can be simply defined as 'the way we do things around here', the new
employee needs time to learn just what this means for

everyday conduct. This is not something that can be dealt with simply by a talk on the first day – it has to be experienced.

There are five main elements to be considered:

- knowledge of the organisation
- understanding the employment package
- social integration
- progress reviews
- probation.

Knowledge of the organisation

To be fully effective, employees need to know how their work fits into the overall pattern of things. This may best be explained on a staged basis:

- first, the way the individual job links with the work of colleagues in the immediate team or section
- then how the work of the team fits into the purpose and activities of the wider department or function
- finally, how the work of the department contributes to the overall aims and activities of the organisation as a whole.

How these explanations are given will vary with the size, structure and type of organisation, but the sequence can be borne in mind by the employee's immediate and senior managers, and some positive steps taken to ensure that all aspects are covered over a period of a few weeks. The first step – the work links within the immediate team – will need to be dealt with at a very early stage. This and the next stage are often best handled by arranging for the employee to follow the work-flow within the team and department. Almost all work in a team or department starts with inputs of information or materials and ends with outputs in terms of completed or part-completed services, processed data or goods. The supervisor or starter's friend can take the new employee through the various processes, preferably by demonstrating what happens at each stage and introducing the other employees involved, rather than merely by a verbal explanation. This may not be practicable for the activities of the organisation as a whole, although short visits to the other main departments and the issue of company publicity and sales literature should certainly be considered.

If the organisation has endorsed a statement of core values, the new employee will need an explanation of how these are expected to be evident in everyday work and in employees' and managers' general conduct. Ideally, an organisation's values so permeate the way everything is done that their formal definition is barely necessary. In most organisations, however, formal statements of values do need reinforcement through publicity, promotion, explanation and the example set by managers.

One other topic that an induction programme should include is the organisation's policy regarding trade union recognition and the role, if applicable, of trade union or employee representatives. The new employee should be introduced to the relevant representative at a fairly early stage and given information about the existence and purpose of works councils or other forms of collective consultation and negotiation. It is helpful to have an understanding with recognised trade unions about the way they approach and recruit new employees into membership, so that managers can tell new employees what to expect – remembering that it is not acceptable for an organisation to put pressure on an employee to join or not join a union.

Understanding the employment package

There are a few key elements of employees' terms and conditions of employment which need to be explained on or before the first day – particularly pay and working times. There are many other elements which, although included in the formal statement of terms and conditions and the contractual documents issued at the time of appointment, need further explanation if new employees are to have a full understanding of their rights, benefits and obligations. Because of the often detailed nature of many of these elements, it is a mistake to attempt to provide a full explanation on the first day. Much of the detail will not be absorbed, and it is only after being in the job for a period that many employees will be able to ask relevant questions. Examples of the topics that generally benefit from later explanation are:

- *pensions* – an important but complicated subject, particularly if the organisation's scheme provides options for various levels of benefit
- *appraisal systems*, their performance or competence criteria, and any link with pay
- *bonus or merit payments, profit-share or share option systems* and the like

- *grievance and disciplinary procedures*
- *training and development* – programmes and opportunities
- *equal opportunity policies* and rules about discriminatory behaviour or harassment
- *health and safety*, beyond those matters covered as a matter of priority on the first day
- *sickness absence procedures*
- *suggestion schemes, award schemes* given for high performance, and the like.

Details of these kinds of item are generally set out in staff handbooks or other documents, but it is helpful for these to be supplemented by oral explanations from personnel staff or supervisors. The new employee should also be actively encouraged to ask questions about anything relating to the employment package, and told who to ask about specific issues such as pensions or occupational health.

Social integration

There is more to any job than understanding its work components and how it relates to the work of others. Working with other people is a social experience, and inclusion or exclusion from the informal groupings that develop within a workforce can have a powerful influence on any employee's feelings of acceptance or rejection. A failure to integrate socially is a not uncommon reason for early leaving. There are formal and informal aspects to this. Formally, there are the social events organised by the employing organisation or its sports or social club. Informally, there are the lunchtime and after-work gatherings of work

31

colleagues in the staff restaurant or in local pubs, wine bars or leisure centres.

Not all new starters may wish to become active in these social events, but unless someone helps to break the ice for those who would enjoy participation, the uncomfortable feeling of being left out can be very persistent. This is another example of induction in which the starter's friend can be particularly helpful. The simple invitation to join a group of colleagues for lunch or a visit to the local fitness centre can do much to make the new employee feel one of the team.

Progress reviews

Whether or not employees are appointed on the basis of a formally designated probationary period, effective induction involves the careful monitoring of their progress during their first few weeks or months, with help being given to resolve any problems that may then arise. Most of the responsibility for this rests with the immediate supervisor or manager who is the person best placed to observe how well the new employee is settling in, and to spot when problems occur.

The extent to which this aspect of induction is formalised will depend partly on whether it is the policy to specify a probationary period in the contract of employment, and partly on the organisation's management style. The more formal the approach, the more necessary it is to operate a system of documented progress checks made at defined intervals. In an informal setting, the process may be left largely to individual supervisors and managers – always provided they understand the importance of careful follow-up and know what to do if there are problems.

There are a number of aspects of a new employee's progress that should be reviewed at regular intervals. These include, particularly:

- *work quality and output.* Is the employee developing the necessary expertise at a satisfactory rate? Is the employee developing or displaying the competencies needed to do the job well? If not, is more intensive training or guidance needed?
- *attitudes.* Is the employee displaying keen interest in the job and an obvious willingness to learn? Or are there indications of boredom, disillusionment, carelessness or other adverse signs – and if there are, what are the reasons and how can improvements be achieved?
- *relationships.* How well is the new employee fitting into the team? What is the quality of the employee/supervisor relationship? If there are any problems, what is the cause and how should these problems be resolved?
- *conduct.* Is the employee's general conduct or behaviour consistent with the standards and style the organisation requires? If not, does the employee need counselling about this, or even an initial warning?
- *attendance.* What is the employee's record regarding absences and daily timekeeping? If this is unsatisfactory, what have been the reasons and what needs to be done to correct the situation?
- *potential.* Is the employee showing any potential for more advanced or different work, or for a possible supervisory or managerial role? If so,

should he or she be nominated for an assessment centre or otherwise noted for consideration for transfer or early promotion?

Managers involved in progress reviews need to be aware of common causes of difficulty during a new employee's first few weeks or months. These can include:

- personality clashes with a member or members of the work group or with the supervisor
- disappointment with the job for a variety of reasons, such as its proving less interesting than the employee expected, or a failure to achieve an expected level of earnings
- worries about the ability to cope if the job is felt to be more difficult than was expected
- personal or domestic problems, such as travel to work arrangements' proving difficult, or overtime or shift requirements' causing problems for childcare arrangements
- for women who join a mainly male workforce, the psychological discomfort and exclusion of working in a 'macho' environment
- the inability to join in social activities after work because of domestic responsibilities
- for ethnic minority employees, the stress caused by working in any organisation in which there is direct or indirect racism (for instance, as exhibited as part of the 'canteen culture').

The emphasis in induction is primarily on helping the new employee adjust to the organisation. But if a number of the issues listed above are identified as causing induction problems, it is the organisation that needs to change. Progress reviews which reveal a pattern of organisational or cultural problems are as valuable an element in organisational development as they are in induction.

For many new employees, the type of help they need in adjusting to life in a different organisational culture is best provided in an informal counselling or mentoring mode. The provision of actual information and practical job training can be organised on a structured basis, with the employee's immediate supervisor or manager playing a leading role. But helping a new employee understand and relate to the organisation's behavioural values and standards may best be given by a perceptive and helpful colleague. The skills involved are those of the counsellor or mentor – encouraging new employees to think through any problems they may have and to evolve their own solutions – though with advice and guidance to ensure success.

Probation

For many jobs, employees are appointed initially on a formal probationary basis, with continued employment beyond the probationary period being dependent on a satisfactory assessment. Some managers see probationary periods as being simply the time in which to weed out employees who fail to come up to standard. Although the use of a trial period for this purpose is clearly legitimate, the objective should always be to achieve a successful outcome, rather than simply to identify failures which have to result in dismissals. The follow-up assistance and progress reviews that are needed for effective induction apply just as much, or possibly more, to employees on formal probation as to those appointed on non-probationary terms.

What is needed in a contractual probation period is a more formal and structured approach to reviews and the assessment which decides whether or not employment should continue. The length of probation should depend on the nature of the job, the duration of any formal job training programme, and the period necessary for an employee to reach an acceptable standard. Probation periods should not be unnecessarily lengthy, as they involve the employee in a period of potential anxiety about the outcome. Probationary periods can, however, be extended if evidence about suitability at the end of the initially defined period is too uncertain to justify a decision either to confirm the employment or to terminate it. The principal criteria for the effective use of formal probationary periods are these:

- Employees must be told very clearly of their employment status and its implications, the duration of the probationary period, the standards they are required to reach to ensure continued employment, and that there will be a series of progress reviews.
- There should be a schedule of these reviews, with a record kept of their content and assessments.
- Supervisors and managers must understand the importance of these reviews and be given guidance as to how to conduct them and on the factors on which assessments are to be made.
- Supervisors and managers should also understand and accept that the primary aim is to ensure that new probationary employees are given the

necessary training and other support to achieve a successful outcome.

- A formal decision about continued employment is made at the end of the probationary period, based on a thorough final assessment which should include an appraisal-type discussion with the employee.
- The employee should be formally notified in writing of the outcome. A common failing is to notify only those cases in which the decision is that the employee has failed to reach the necessary standard. It is just as important to confirm successful outcomes.
- If the decision is that probation should be extended, this, and the reasons for it, should be explained to the employee and confirmed in writing.

Employees on probation – as with new employees generally – can be helped by knowing who they can approach in addition to their immediate supervisor about any difficulties or concerns that may arise. While, for employees at large, this can be organised on an informal basis (an orally arranged starter's friend), it may be helpful in the more formal context of a contractual probationary appointment for this to be documented. An example of a paragraph in a letter of appointment is given below, together with an example of a confirmation of the successful completion of probation and of a probationary period being extended.

Example of the probationary elements in an appointment letter:

> This appointment is on a probationary basis for an initial period of six months, although this may be extended if it is decided that more time is necessary to assess your suitability for continued employment. Your progress will be subject to monthly reviews, which your manager will discuss with you. A final review will be conducted within the two weeks before the probationary period ends and you will be told in writing of the outcome.
>
> Throughout the probationary period, your manager will ensure that you receive all the necessary training and support, and will explain to you the standards you will be expected to achieve. In addition to help from your manager, [......X......] has been assigned to help you with any problems you may experience. S/he is there to help you and it is important that you take full advantage of this arrangement. If you are ever in any doubt about anything involved in your work, do ask – do not guess or allow any concerns to remain unresolved. The aim is to ensure that you complete your probation successfully.

Example of a letter confirming the successful completion of probation:

> Following your recent final assessment, I am pleased to tell you that you have completed your probationary period successfully. I can therefore confirm your continued employment on a normal basis in accordance with the attached revised contract of employment.

Example of a letter confirming a decision to extend probation:

> Your probationary period is due to end on [...date....]. However, you will know from our recent discussions that we need to see a sustained improvement in the following aspects of your work: [give details]. In view of this it is not yet possible to confirm your continued employment. We have therefore decided that your probationary period should be extended to [....date....]. If you achieve and maintain a satisfactory standard during this period, your continued employment will then be confirmed. We hope very much that this will be the outcome, and we shall provide the necessary further training which, together with your own efforts, should enable you to complete your probation successfully. I must, however, place on record that if you fail to meet the requirements of the job, your employment will have to be terminated.

KEY POINTS

- Induction does not end with the first day. Acquiring a full understanding of the organisation and acclimatising to the culture of the organisation may take several months. An effective induction programme takes this into account.
- The aim should be a planned expansion of the employee's understanding of the purpose, values and activities of the organisation and of the elements in the employment package, and action to help the employee's social integration.

- Knowledge of the organisation should begin with the way the job fits into the work of the team, then how the team's role contributes to the purpose and activity of the wider department, and finally how the department contributes to the aims and activities of the organisation as a whole.

- Some elements in the employment package need to be explained on the first day (eg time-recording) but others, such as pensions or performance bonuses, are best explained later.

- The supervisor and starter's friend may need to help the new employee integrate socially in order to prevent feelings of rejection or isolation.

- The new employee's progress needs to be carefully monitored during the first few weeks or months. If appointments are made on a formal probationary basis, this monitoring may include documented reviews – but in any event, the supervisor or manager should regularly check how the new employee is progressing in terms of work quality, attitude, relationships, conduct, attendance and potential.

- Employees appointed on a formal probationary basis should be told what they need to do to achieve the satisfactory completion of their probationary period, helped to be successful, and informed formally of their transfer from probationary to normal employment status.

5

Do some groups of employees have particular induction needs?

- ☑ School leavers
- ☑ Graduates
- ☑ Part-timers and job-sharers
- ☑ Home-based workers
- ☑ Returners from career breaks
- ☑ People with disabilities
- ☑ Ethnic minority employees
- ☑ Employees dealing with the general public
- ☑ Employees with caring responsibilities
- ☑ Newly appointed supervisors and managers

Although the general principles and processes of induction described in previous chapters apply to all new employees, there are some groups or types of employees who have special needs. They are listed in the box above, and each will be examined in turn.

School leavers

Most school leavers – unlike most adult starters – have no experience of paid employment. Their induction consequently needs to be seen as an entry to the world of work – not just to a new job with a new employer. Because of this, they are likely to require more help with understanding the need for a self-disciplined approach to compliance with attendance requirements and the organisation's general rules and regulations. Other points to consider include:

- an early assessment of each individual's learning capabilities and attitudes to work, as some may require more help than others in developing the necessary job competencies and adapting to a work culture
- a particular emphasis on health and safety aspects
- the possible need for training in core competencies, such as literacy, numeracy and problem-solving skills
- advice and encouragement to embark on courses of study leading to vocational qualifications, such as relevant NVQs.

Graduates

Some graduates, like school leavers, may have no previous work experience, though many will have had vacation employment. In addition to gaining knowledge of the subjects they have studied, they should have developed a higher level of competence than school leavers in intellectual analysis and self-directed learning. The implications for their induction are these:

- They are likely to be more enquiring about the broad commercial or organisational context of their jobs – such as the nature of the market, economic trends, and the role of their employing organisation in the relevant sector.
- They can be encouraged to research much of this information for themselves, rather than having it all given to them through more conventional training methods.

For example, as an induction training exercise, a new graduate employee could be given the task of identifying and analysing market trends, producing a report and presenting this to senior management. Some help could be provided in identifying sources of data and in the provision of company statistics, but the graduate would have to use initiative in extending this information. Writing and presenting the report would also be an excellent way of assessing and developing the employee's written and oral communication skills.

Part-timers and job-sharers

New part-time employees, including job-sharers, have the same induction needs as full-time workers. However, they are sometimes left out of induction programmes, partly because they may not be at work at the times when formal induction courses are being run and partly through the mistaken attitude of some managers that part-timers are in some way less important. Neither of these reasons is acceptable. Part-time employment has become an increasingly widespread and normal component of today's more flexible workforce, and it is essential that new part-time employees are integrated as quickly into the organisation as their full-time colleagues. The issue is therefore largely logistical – organising for their induction training to take place during their normal hours of attendance.

So far as specific topics are concerned, one aspect that may need careful explanation is the way various employee benefits or terms of employment, such as annual leave, overtime premiums and pensions, are calculated on a pro rata basis to those applying to full-time employees. Job-sharing arrangements also need explanation – particularly the implications of two job-sharers being jointly responsible for the whole job and for ensuring satisfactory mutual briefing and handover arrangements. (See *Part-Time Workers* by Anna Allan and Lucy Daniels in this series for more information on the subject.)

Home-based workers

IT and communication developments are leading to a steady increase in the number of employees who work from their homes. Because their attendance at their organisations' workplaces is infrequent or sporadic, there is a danger that very little attention will be given to their induction. There is then a serious risk that they will not have a sufficient understanding of how their work relates to that of their office-based colleagues or to the organisation's business plans. They may also feel isolated and worry about being ill-informed about events and developments at work. Several measures can help the new home-based worker, both in the very early stages of employment and on a longer-term basis:

- They should be sent all the communications which they would have received had they been based in the workplace – reports, notices, memos, house journals and the like – even if some of these are not directly relevant to their work. Additionally, if home-workers are employed in any numbers, a special newsletter for them can prove particularly helpful in keeping them in touch with the organisation and each other. E-mail can be a very useful medium for two-way communication and information.
- At a very early stage, there should be a visit to the workplace to meet the staff who will be involved in sending and receiving their work, and generally to see how the organisation operates.
- Their supervisors should visit them at home to discuss progress and conduct the same periodic induction reviews as for office-based staff.
- They should be invited to attend all of the organisation's social events.
- They should be encouraged to 'drop into the office for a chat' at any time, with a particular emphasis on talking to the personnel staff about any personal problems.

New homeworkers may also need training in the use of any equipment with which they may be provided – such as PCs, special telephone links, and the like.

Returners from career breaks

It is sometimes assumed that employees returning after career breaks (such as those taken while bringing up a family) do not need any induction training because they already have the necessary work experience. But if the break has been of a significant duration there will almost certainly have been changes in many aspects of the work, and probably in the management structure and decision-making process. Personalities will also have changed. There may also be a need for new or more highly developed skills, such as for fast-moving IT applications. An individual induction plan is therefore needed for each of the returners to bring them up to date about changes since they were last employed.

People with disabilities

Discussions should take place in the pre-employment period with new recruits who have disabilities about the adjustments or aids that may be necessary to enable them to work effectively. These may include;

- hearing loops, Braille keyboards, or readers for those with impaired sight
- other adaptations specific to the particular equipment used in the job
- wheelchair access
- safety arrangements, such as ensuring assistance with rapid escape in the event of fire.

Aids and arrangements of these kinds need explanation and demonstration immediately employment starts, together with a check that the disabled employee can take a full part in any specific induction activities. Supervisors and the employee's colleagues may also need training and guidance about the effects of some forms of disability, such as epilepsy, and ways of communicating with people with impaired hearing.

Ethnic minority employees

New employees from ethnic minorities are likely to be particularly sensitive to the individual and group attitudes of their fellow workers and managers, and to the general culture of the workplace. Personnel managers, and managers at large, should be alert to any form of direct racism or the unintended but adverse effects of stereotyping. Apart from this general factor, some language training may be needed for those with limited knowledge of English, together with the provision of information about conditions of employment and company rules and regulations in new recruits' first language. An explanation of the jargon of the trade may also be necessary, though this may apply equally to recruits from the majority population.

Employees dealing with the general public

New employees whose work immediately involves contact with customers and the general public (such as many teleworkers, receptionists and retail staff) will need very early advice or training in their induction about how the organisation wants them to behave. There will probably be rules about how to respond to telephone calls, what to do if a customer is upset or abusive, who particular queries or complaints should be referred to, and the general tenor of the organisation's customer care policies.

Employees with caring responsibilities

New employees who are involved for the first time in work that involves care for the young or frail require intensive early training in the responsibilities and skills involved. Pre-employment checks are legally necessary for work with children, but these simply screen out those whose criminal records make them unacceptable carers. What is needed for those who are cleared by this preliminary screening is a very full explanation of the duties, rights and obligations involved in the work, and training and counselling to develop the necessary skills and attitudes. Ongoing reviews of the employee's ability to understand and apply the principles of sensitive and effective care are vital, with every kind of support being given to help overcome the problems and stress that this type of work frequently entails. Because the welfare of those being cared for has to take priority, these are occupations from which employees who fail to acquire or demonstrate the essential qualities must be removed at a much earlier stage than would be acceptable for many other occupations.

Newly appointed supervisors and managers

Because managers are usually appointed individually, often involving internal promotions, their induction requirements are often overlooked. Yet their full effectiveness can generally be achieved far more quickly if such needs are recognised. Their principal induction requirements are usually:

- to get to know the relevant formal and informal hierarchies and decision-making processes
- to meet their immediate seniors and subordinate staff, and the managers of other departments or functions with whom their jobs interact
- to understand the expectations of other managers to be consulted or kept informed about events or decisions – even when the formal procedures appear to permit unilateral action
- to identify the best sources of relevant information and advice, both within the organisation and externally.

It is consequently very useful for an individual induction programme to be arranged, which will probably include:

- the issue of a package of relevant reports, organisation charts, business plans, correspondence files, minutes of meetings, and the like
- an annotated list of the key personalities, internal and external, with whom the job will involve contact
- briefing sessions by the immediate senior manager and the personnel manager about all aspects of the job and of the organisation's ways of working
- a programme of visits to other parts of the

organisation and perhaps to key customers or clients

- opportunities to sit in and observe various management meetings.

Even with this kind of planned preparation, new managers are still likely to make some mistakes or errors of judgement in their early months. Their seniors should use discussions of these incidents positively, taking the approach 'What can you learn from this?', rather than allocating blame or treating mistakes as potential disciplinary matters.

KEY POINTS

- Some types of employees have induction needs beyond those applying to all new employees.
- School leavers have to adjust to the world of work, and need support in developing the self-discipline involved in complying with attendance requirements and other work disciplines.
- Graduates may be more enquiring about the whole organisational context of their jobs, and can be encouraged to research some of this information for themselves.
- Part-timers have the same induction needs as full-time staff, but induction programmes need to take account of their more limited time availability for induction activities.

- Home-based workers need an understanding of how their work relates to that of their office-based colleagues, together with a flow of information to keep them in touch with workplace developments.
- Staff returning from career breaks need refresher training to catch up with changes in techniques and the way work is organised.
- People with disabilities may need aids and adjustments to the workplace to assist both in job training and in meeting safety requirements.
- In monitoring the progress of new ethnic minority employees, managers need to be alert to the possibility of racial stereotyping or harassment.
- New employees in jobs involving personal care (eg for children or the elderly) require early training in the necessary skills, and must be monitored for any indications of unsuitable conduct or attitude.
- Newly appointed managers need help in understanding the formal and informal hierarchies within which their jobs are located, and the decision-making processes to which they must conform.

How should induction courses be organised?

- ☑ Choosing the course attenders
- ☑ Scheduling the course
- ☑ The course content
- ☑ Induction training methods
- ☑ Who does what

When a sufficient number of new employees join an organisation at the same time (or within a short period) most of the early induction requirements can be met by organising an induction training course. This saves time by avoiding the repetition of the same information to new employees individually, and ensures that all the starters receive the same (and correct) information in the same format. However, there are some potential dangers:

- Managers may assume that induction has been completed simply by a new employee's course attendance, and that there is no more they need to do. It is very important that the induction course is seen only as a useful start to induction, and that ongoing assistance in the workplace and periodic progress reviews are still needed.

- New employees may experience a surfeit of information if too much material is packed into a single training event at the beginning of employment.
- New employees cannot experience the working culture of the organisation while attending a course. They may be told about the organisation's values and standards, but only by being in the actual workplace will they fully understand 'the way we do things around here'.
- On a highly organised course, the participants may be so spoon-fed that their transfer to a less organised workplace may constitute the very kind of culture shock that induction is intended to prevent.

But provided these dangers are recognised, formal, off-the-job induction courses can play a valuable part in helping groups of new employees to settle in quickly.

There are several factors that need to be considered in planning an induction course:

- Who should attend?
- How should the course be scheduled?
- What topics should the course include?
- What training methods or techniques should be used?
- Who should act as course tutors or contributors?

Choosing the course attenders

The main choice in deciding who should attend is between limiting attendance to employees in the same job or occupation, or involving all new employees joining within a set period, whatever their jobs. The advantage of single occupational groups is that the course content can be specific to the jobs involved, but this type of course is practicable only when the organisation recruits same-job employees in groups. Multi-occupational groups are more common and these can help to promote mutual understanding across all the organisation's departments or functions. A related issue is whether it is satisfactory to mix new employees from different levels – skilled professionals with basic grade workers, managers with non-managers.

The best approach, if the numbers of new employees permit, can be to bring a large mixed group together for general information topics, and to use smaller single-occupation groups for more detailed topics specific to particular types of work.

Scheduling the course

There are three main issues to decide when planning the structure of an induction course:

- its duration
- whether it should be continuous, or divided into modules
- its timing relative to the starting dates of new employees.

The length of a course is largely dependent on its content –

the range and scale of the material it is to include. At its most basic, this may consist of no more than essential first-day information and consequently require only about half a day; while a much more comprehensive programme may require as many as five days.

There is a danger that a comprehensive course will attempt too much too soon if, for example, it takes up the whole of the first week of employment. If the course is to include a lot of material which may not be of immediate relevance to new employees, it is best to deliver it on a modular basis over a period of several weeks – say, one day a week for five weeks, or ten half-days over ten weeks. The content can then start with the most immediately relevant topics and gradually be opened out to include more general information. The induction material can also be phased if it is integrated with a period of several weeks' job training.

Some organisations run induction courses at set times throughout the year – monthly or quarterly, for example – and arrange attendance on each course for all those employees who have started since the previous course. The problem with this arrangement is that some employees will have been at work for several weeks before they can attend, and this is very unsatisfactory unless matters of immediate importance are dealt with by some other procedure. There may be logistical benefits in organising induction courses at set times, but it is then important for first-day induction, covering the topics described in Chapter 3, to be arranged on an individual basis. The course can then concentrate on matters of more general or longer-term interest.

The course content

It should be recognised that an induction course cannot address every relevant issue. It can be an extremely useful and effective way of explaining a range of material common to the interests of all employees, but this will still leave some matters to be dealt with on an individual basis within each employee's workplace. Supervisors and managers need to know what the course covers, and consequently what issues are still their responsibility. The checklist in the Appendix can be used to decide which items should be in the course – with the emphasis being on those that all employees need to know about, whatever their particular jobs. This is likely to include:

- the pay system
- conditions of service and employee benefits
- general health, safety and security matters
- training and development policies
- trade unions and employee consultation
- the organisation's mission, aims and values
- the organisation's structure
- information about the industry or sector.

Induction training methods

Inevitably, much induction training consists of imparting information. The scope for course attenders to be actively involved is much less than in skills training, and there is consequently a danger of boredom and inattention if the course consists solely of a series of talks. A range of training methods is needed to create the variety that will hold employees' attention. Methods that can be used in addition to 'chalk and talk' include:

- *films and videos*. Useful for showing aspects of the organisation's activities which may not be readily accessible for the course attenders to visit, and to show them the organisation's publicity material.
- *tape/slide packages*. Cheaper to produce than films or videos and therefore more readily adaptable for specific induction purposes.
- *visits*. Guided visits around the organisation's premises and to see the various processes are far more effective than explanatory talks. They also help new employees to learn the geography of complex sites.
- *documentation*. Employee handbooks, publicity material, annual reports and the like, together with specially prepared handouts, all help to reinforce or illustrate information relayed.
- *practical demonstrations*. These may be possible for subjects such as safety hazards, fire precautions, production methods and IT systems.
- *discussion groups*. A useful way of stimulating interest in the organisation's policies and procedures. For example, a session on customer care in a retail setting might begin with the question for discussion: 'Why do you think we exchange returned goods without question?'
- *projects*. With some groups it may be possible to include an element of self-learning – for example, giving teams of three or four new employees the task of examining several years' annual reports and producing a summary of trends to be presented at a later module of the course.

Conventional talks should use visual aids (OHPs, slides, charts, etc) and managers contributing to the courses should have training in presentational skills.

Who does what

One way of providing variety in an induction course is to involve a number of different contributors. Very short courses dealing with only basic employment data may well be handled entirely by a single personnel officer, though even in a half-day course, an introductory welcome by a senior manager is desirable. In longer courses, it is even more important that course attenders encounter more than just one or two speakers. Who might be suitable will depend on the size and structure of the organisation, but the following checklist can be used to consider the possibilities:

- *The chief executive or most senior manager* – particularly to give a short introductory welcome and highlight the key characteristics of the organisation.
- *Heads of departments* – to describe the role of their various functions.
- *Safety officer* – to explain and demonstrate health and safety matters.
- *Training manager* – to explain training and development policies and opportunities.
- *Medical adviser or occupational health nurse* – to explain health policies and accident procedures.
- *Trade union officer or elected employee representative* – to explain the role of any collective employee machinery from the employees' viewpoint.

- *Payroll/pensions manager* – to explain pay and pensions systems.
- *IT systems manager or specialist* – to describe the organisation's IT policy, the internal e-mail system, and access to the Internet.
- *Sports and social club secretary* – to describe and promote the use of social and sports facilities.
- A *'front-line' employee* – to describe what day-to-day work involves.

The personnel department normally has overall responsibility for the planning and administration of the course, and also (as a minimum) for conducting the sessions on terms and conditions of employment. The department should also monitor the effectiveness of the whole induction process, including ensuring that ongoing progress reviews are conducted, recorded and acted on.

KEY POINTS

- Induction courses are useful when a number of new employees can be grouped together for induction training.
- Attendance at an induction course still needs to be supplemented by induction activities in the workplace, including social integration and adaptation to the organisational culture.
- To avoid too intensive an input of information, induction courses can be scheduled on a modular basis with short sessions spread over several weeks.

- Subjects particularly suitable for inclusion in an induction course programme are the pay system, pension scheme, training and development policies and opportunities, general health and safety matters, grievance and disciplinary procedures, and the organisation's mission, core values and business aims.
- To maintain interest, a variety of training methods should be used in addition to 'chalk and talk'. These may include films, videos, discussion groups, visits to worksites and practical demonstrations.
- A range of contributors to induction courses can also provide variety, and may include senior managers, safety and training officers, medical advisers, payroll and pensions officers and front-line employees.
- A checklist can be used to decide which elements of induction to include in the course, and to allocate responsibility for each session.

How does induction relate to other people management processes?

Induction is not a self-contained process and should not be planned in isolation. Both in content and style, it needs to be consistent with other aspects of people management and contribute to the broader objective of securing a competent and committed workforce. The most relevant links are as follows:

- *Recruitment and selection.* Assessments of how well new employees perform in their jobs provide valuable information about the effectiveness of the recruitment and selection process. Are the best kinds of people being recruited? Are the selection criteria valid? Answers to questions of these kinds can be provided by analysing the correlation between predictions of suitability made at the time of selection and the periodic reviews of new employees' performance standards.
- *Investors in People.* The IIP standard includes a requirement for a training plan which applies to all employees and links training and development to the needs of the organisation's business plan.

Induction is an essential element of this plan. The emphasis in IIP on employees' understanding organisational aims and achievements, and the way each job contributes to the wider picture, implies that induction training – whether formal or informal – should include information and explanations of the organisation's objectives, values and progress.

- *Legal aspects.* While there is no statutory requirement to provide induction training, the fairness of a dismissal for failing to reach necessary standards may be examined by an Employment Tribunal. If the dismissal took place at the end of a protracted probationary period, one of the matters a tribunal is likely to examine is the extent to which the employee was provided with guidance and training and told about the targets or standards which had to be met.

- *Performance or competence appraisals.* Organisations operating any form of appraisal system need to use the progress reviews carried out during induction to include assessment and discussion of the same performance and competence criteria as apply in subsequent appraisals.

- *Employee assistance programmes.* Some organisations operate in-house or bought-in confidential counselling and welfare services. During induction, the purpose of these services and how to access them should be explained. They may be of particular help to any new employee who experiences personal problems either in coping or coming to terms with a different organisational culture, or who is experiencing domestic problems because of the new working arrangements.

● *Skills training.* Induction elements can be included within a skills training programme. More generally, the messages given out by the way in which induction is delivered (perhaps by an emphasis on discussion and questioning) need to be similar to those implied by the nature and style of any skills training. Explanations during induction of the organisation's various functions and the types of work and jobs involved will also help employees on skills training programmes to relate their training to the wider organisational scene.

● *Lifelong learning* (including continuing professional development). Neither new employees nor their managers should assume that the completion of induction and any initial skills training marks the conclusion of training activities. Induction should be used to encourage acceptance of the concept of lifelong learning and to stimulate employees' interest in beginning courses of study and taking a large measure of responsibility for their own personal and career development.

One of the ways of providing support and encouragement for this ongoing process is the establishment of learning resource centres – a room or rooms within the organisation stocked with a wide range of self-learning material and information about courses of study and equipped with PCs and probably Internet access. Training videos, learning programmes on interactive CDs, technical and managerial books and journals – material of these kinds can be made available for employees to use during lunch breaks or after work, or to borrow. As part of their induction, new employees should have a guided visit to the centre where some of the material can be demonstrated, and told what the procedures are for making use of the centre for self-directed learning.

KEY POINTS
- Induction should be co-ordinated with other aspects of people management. These include
  - recruitment and selection
  - Investors in People
  - legal aspects of employment
  - performance or competence appraisal
  - employee assistance programmes
  - skills training
  - lifelong learning.
- A learning resource centre can encourage employees to continue the learning process after completion of formal induction, and an explanation of the use and purpose of such a centre should be included in the induction programme.

Appendix: An induction checklist

This checklist can be used to decide what items to include in an induction programme, which may be suitable for inclusion in an induction course, who should be responsible for each item, and by when information or guidance should be given. Not all the topics listed will apply to all organisations, while additional specialist items may be necessary in specific industries or functions.

Topic
Reception

Initial reception

by whom:
by when:

Initial documentation:
P45

by whom:
by when:

NI number

| by whom: |
| by when: |

Bank account details

| by whom: |
| by when: |

Next of kin

| by whom: |
| by when: |

Issue of:
ID/security pass

| by whom: |
| by when: |

car park permit

| by whom: |
| by when: |

staff handbook

| by whom: |
| by when: |

Introduction to supervisor or manager

by whom:
by when:

Topic
Site geography and facilities

General tour of the site

by whom:
by when:

Cloakrooms and lavatories

by whom:
by when:

Staff restaurant and vending machines

by whom:
by when:

Car/motor cycle/bicycle parking

by whom:
by when:

Notice boards

by whom:
by when:

Employee's work location

by whom:
by when:

Fire exits

by whom:
by when:

First aid room/first aid boxes

by whom:
by when:

Time recording equipment

by whom:
by when:

Issue of equipment:

by whom:
by when:

protective clothing

by whom:	
by when:	

pager/mobile phone

by whom:	
by when:	

Topic
Health and safety

Fire and emergency drills

by whom:	
by when:	

Security alerts

by whom:	
by when:	

General safety rules

by whom:	
by when:	

Specific hazards (eg toxic chemicals)

by whom:
by when:

Smoking regulations

by whom:
by when:

Accident procedures

by whom:
by when:

Hygiene regulations

by whom:
by when:

Introduction to workplace safety representative

by whom:
by when:

Introduction to workplace first-aider

by whom:
by when:

Occupational health service

by whom:
by when:

Topic
Pay

Pay system:
basic pay

by whom:
by when:

bonus schemes

by whom:
by when:

grading/job evaluation

by whom:
by when:

Allowances (shift, overtime, standby, etc)

by whom:
by when:

Deductions (savings schemes, etc)

by whom:
by when:

Explanation of payslip

by whom:
by when:

Method of payment

by whom:
by when:

Topic
Other conditions, benefits and employment policies

Attendance: hours of work, flexitime, meal/rest breaks

by whom:
by when:

Leave: entitlement, notification

by whom:
by when:

Sick pay: notification of absence, entitlements

by whom:	
by when:	

Extra-statutory holidays

by whom:	
by when:	

Pension scheme and life assurance

by whom:	
by when:	

Company cars

by whom:	
by when:	

Expenses: entitlements and claims procedure

by whom:	
by when:	

Private medical/dental insurance

by whom:	
by when:	

Staff purchases/discounts etc

by whom:
by when:

Maternity/paternity leave

by whom:
by when:

Company loans (season tickets, mortgages, etc)

by whom:
by when:

Any flexibility in choice of benefits

by whom:
by when:

Social, sports, fitness facilities

by whom:
by when:

Counselling and welfare scheme

by whom:
by when:

Disciplinary rules and procedure

by whom:
by when:

Grievance procedure

by whom:
by when:

Equal opportunity policy

by whom:
by when:

Alcohol/substance abuse policy

by whom:
by when:

Disability policy and equipment

by whom:
by when:

Anti-harassment/bullying policy and procedure

by whom:
by when:

Customer care and contact policies and procedures

| *by whom:* |
| *by when:* |

Code of conduct (organisational ethics, anti-corruption, etc)

| *by whom:* |
| *by when:* |

Topic
Workplace matters

Introduction to team/colleagues

| *by whom:* |
| *by when:* |

Introduction to 'starter's friend'

| *by whom:* |
| *by when:* |

Internal communications (e-mail, Intranet, pagers, etc)

| *by whom:* |
| *by when:* |

Rules about private use of telephones, faxes, PCs, etc

| *by whom:* |
| *by when:* |

Data protection, confidentiality regulations

| *by whom:* |
| *by when:* |

Password access to IT systems

| *by whom:* |
| *by when:* |

Care of equipment, back-up of computer data, etc

| *by whom:* |
| *by when:* |

Introduction to job trainer/mentor

| *by whom:* |
| *by when:* |

Issue of job/equipment manuals

| *by whom:* |
| *by when:* |

Topic
Appraisal, training and development

Performance/competence appraisal system

by whom:
by when:

Individual training plans

by whom:
by when:

Relevant training programmes (NVQs, etc)

by whom:
by when:

Assistance with personal study

by whom:
by when:

Topic

Employee involvement and communication

Introduction to workplace employee/trade union representative

by whom:
by when:

Trade union recognition

by whom:
by when:

Relevant collective agreements

by whom:
by when:

Joint consultative system

by whom:
by when:

Briefing group system

by whom:
by when:

Suggestion scheme

| *by whom:* |
| *by when:* |

Award schemes (eg for sales performance)

| *by whom:* |
| *by when:* |

Issue of staff newsletter, recent notices, etc

| *by whom:* |
| *by when:* |

Topic
The organisation and its industry or sector

Issue of company literature:
sales

| *by whom:* |
| *by when:* |

publicity material

| *by whom:* |
| *by when:* |

annual report

by whom:
by when:

house journal

by whom:
by when:

Mission statement and core values

by whom:
by when:

Business plan

by whom:
by when:

Organisational structure/departments/functions, management hierarchy – who's who

by whom:
by when:

The organisation's function (goods/services, etc)

by whom:
by when:

Brief organisational history

by whom:
by when:

Ownership, sources of funding

by whom:
by when:

Relationships with other organisations
(partnerships, local/central government, etc)

by whom:
by when:

Nature and size of the industry or sector

by whom:
by when:

Relevant legislation (regulatory bodies, standards,
etc

by whom:
by when: